We come together as one

Helping Families Grieve, Share, and Heal
The Kate's Club Way

Other books by Nancy Kriseman

The Mindful Caregiver: Finding Ease in the Caregiving Journey. 2014.

Meaningful Connections: Positive Ways To Be Together When A Loved One Has Dementia. 2017.

We come together as one

Helping Families Grieve, Share, and Heal
The Kate's Club Way

Lane Pease Hendricks, MS

Nancy L. Kriseman, LCSW

Published by Kate's Club

Kriseman, Nancy, author and Lane Pease Hendricks, author.

We Come Together as One: Helping Families Grieve, Share and Heal. The Kate's Club Way / by Nancy L Kriseman, Lane Pease Hendricks

p. cm.

"A easy to read book with ideas and information on how to support children and teens who have had a sibling or parent die."
1. Parent death
2. Sibling death
3. Grief and Loss
4. Self-care-death
5. Parenting
6. Supporting children and teens around death

ISBN Paperback: 978-1-7369972-0-8
ISBN Electronic Book: 978-1-7369972-1-5

Printed in the United States of America

The Kate's Club Story

Kate's Club was founded in 2003 by Kate Atwood in Atlanta, Georgia. Kate's own grief story inspired her to create a safe place where children could grieve, share, and heal as well as have fun with others.

Kate's mother died when she was 12 years old. She did not know anyone else who had experienced the death of a parent. In her own family, her father, brother, and Kate all experienced their grief separately and though they loved each other they did not know how to grieve together. Kate threw herself into school and sports but did not get a chance to process her grief. When she founded Kate's Club, she wanted children to find a place where bereaved children could connect with another and share their feelings but also have fun together.

Kate's Club quickly grew into much more. What started with 6 kids going bowling has evolved into social, recreational, and therapeutic support for the whole family serving more than 5000 children and teens since 2003.

Kate Atwood and Kate's Club children

Acknowledgments

The authors would like to extend our gratitude first, to Kate Atwood, for her vision for creating a place for grieving children and their families.

To all the children, teens and families who are members of Kate's Club. They demonstrate so much courage, love, and strength as they process their grief. We have learned so much about grief from them and feel honored that they are willing to let us join in their journey.

We appreciate the staff at Kate's Club who work lovingly and tirelessly to provide a safe space and creative activities for the Kate's Club members.

We are grateful to Kate's Club board of directors who provide so much behind the scenes support.

We are thankful for our wonderful editor, Lydia Gomez, who in addition to being a buddy, volunteered to edit our book.

Most notably, we are indebted to the volunteers, the Kate's Club buddies and ambassadors, who ensure that Kate's Club will continue to thrive.

Lastly, our creative and talented graphic designer, Ines Kuhn, who helped design our cover and formatted our information. She helped "birth" the Kate's Club book!

Introduction

> **Kate's Club's vision is to create a world in which it is okay to grieve.**

After the death of a parent, grandparent, caregiver, or sibling, the life of a child is suddenly and forever changed. The life of the family is unequivocally changed as well. While we all will be confronted with different kinds of change in our lives, death is a big game changer. Children and teens who experience the death of a parent, sibling, or caregiver face enormous challenges as they navigate life without that person.

How This Book Can Be Helpful And Support You

This book provides ideas, information, and support to adults who are caring for children and teens as they journey through their own unique grieving process. The key word is "unique," as each child or teen will process their grief in their own way. There may be a child who refuses to talk about the death, while another child is constantly talking about the loss. As children grow and develop, their cognitive awareness changes. They are more able to deeply process their grief and begin to make meaning of their loss. This journey can indeed take a lifetime.

What makes this book different from others is that it incorporates a unique approach to supporting children, teens, and their families, which we call, "The Kate's Club Way." The Kate's Club Way believes in empowering children and teens as they move through their grief process.

It is our hope that the information and ideas provided in this book will better equip you to provide the support children and teens need. We want them to not only survive the trauma that death can bring forth, but also find ways to thrive.

Table of Contents

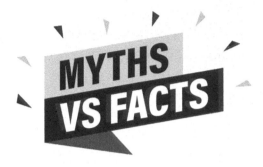

Myths and Misconceptions About Grief

Before we provide the chapters in this book, we wanted to make you aware of the many myths and misconceptions about grief. We want to make sure adults are aware of these because many are a result of our society's discomfort with death.

 At Kate's Club we talk openly and honestly about grief, then everyone in the family will have a better understanding and accept it as a normal part of life.

- Often you will hear people say, "Aren't you over him/her yet?"

- "Why are you so upset? You didn't like him anyway!"

- "It's been several months already, and my ten-year-old daughter keeps bringing up how much she misses her father. I am worried she is not coping well."

- "I cannot cry in front of my children. I have to be strong."

- "My son who is fifteen stays in his room all the time. I am concerned he is not over the loss of his mother. It's been over three months!"

- It is okay to grieve. Grief is a normal response to loss.

- You can grieve over the loss of someone you didn't have a good relationship with. Grief can be an expression of your pain and anguish.

- Children's grief comes and goes, and it's healthy when children express their feelings.

- Crying is a natural reaction to grief. Showing emotions in front of children is okay.

- Teens are at a stage of their lives where they are trying to create some distance and independence from adults. It is not necessarily unusual for teens to stay in their rooms as they may be trying to process their own grief. However, you should check in with them and see if they will express how they are feeling.

Time heals all wounds

- How many times have people said to you, "With time you will feel much better and miss him/her less?"
- Our society has an expectation that as time passes, you will eventually stop grieving.

- As this title suggests, grief does come in waves throughout our lives, and that is normal.
- It's important to let children and teens know that their pain and sadness will come and go and usually does lessen with time.
- Children and teens will revisit their grief throughout their life and be able to process it more deeply as they get older.

There is a right and wrong way to grieve

- Our society has certain expectations about how you "should" grieve and how long it "should" take. Below are some common comments:
- "Mom, I haven't seen you cry. Aren't you upset?"
- "What's wrong with me, Dad? I keep dreaming about Mom, and it's been over a year."

- "You were divorced from him. You should be relieved that he died."
- "I'm worried about my eleven-year-old child. Every time we talk about his mother who died, he starts crying."
- "I'm worried about my child. She has hardly cried."

There is only one way to grieve: your way! Much of the way adults grieve depends on many factors such as:

- Your relationship to the person who died
- How the person died
- Your spiritual beliefs
- Your religious beliefs
- Your own personality
- Your family or cultural beliefs
- Your social support system

So much of the way children and teens grieve depends on many factors as well, such as:

- Their relationship to the person who died
- How the person died
- Your child's developmental understanding of the death
- Whether your child/teen was able to attend the funeral
- How the adults in their life model their own grieving process
- Your child's personality
- Preexistent mental health conditions

The loss can be replaced

- As adults, it is difficult to see your children and teens in despair and sadness.
- There is a tendency to want to comfort them by saying things like:
    - " Don't worry. I will be both mom and dad now."
    - "I have remarried. You have a new mom now, so you won't have to be so sad anymore."
    - "I know you miss your sister, but you now have a new baby sibling."

- No one can replace a parent, sibling, or grandparent.
- Children and teens can foster new relationships, but those new relationships do not take the place of the one with the person who died.

It's better to keep your grief to yourself. Keep busy, and it won't be so hard

- Our culture tends to believe it's best to hurry through your grief, or to just to deny it, and it will go away.
- Adults may think keeping children busy with activities will distract them from their grief.

- Keeping busy does not get rid of your grief but temporarily brushes it aside.
- Ignoring your grief can result in complicated grief, which can interfere in all areas of your life.
- There is no way around grief, only through it. Many people who do not allow themselves to grieve may find themselves having very strong grief reactions even years later.

Children don't grieve

- Children are too young to understand and process grief.
- "Be glad your child is so young. They will bounce back more quickly."

- Children including infants can feel attachment and have grief reactions even though they may not have the words to express their feelings.
- Children tend to grieve differently than adults. They may not always show their grief right away or show their grief the way adults do or expect them to do.
- Children may have what are called grief bursts, which happen sporadically, and soon thereafter, go back to their normal behavior.
- Children may express their feelings through play or behavior.

MYTH 7

It's easier to accept a death after a prolonged illness

- There is a common belief that because the death was expected, you will have an easier time coping with the death.

FACTS

- Each death brings grief, sadness, and pain, no matter how long the person was ill.
- A prolonged illness, though, does give you the opportunity to say goodbye.
- It can also provide you with the opportunity to work through anticipatory grief.
- Children can show trauma reactions after the death from a long illness.
  - They may not have understood the person would die.
  - Often, their lives have been upended by the process of the long illness.
- For some, a prolonged illness can cause feelings related to a term called, overdue death.
  - Overdue death is when a person has suffered for a long time with an illness, and both the person who is ill and the family are ready for the ill person to die. This type of grief can also take a toll on the family.

Chapter One

Grief Waves: Defining Grief, Loss, Mourning And Bereavement

> "Grief is not the enemy, unresolved grief is."
>
> -Kate Atwood, Founder of Kate's Club

Defining Grief, Loss, Bereavement and Mourning

In this section you will learn the different terms about grief so that you can better understand how to support yourself, and your children and teens.

Loss

The reaction to losing something that has great meaning and value to you.

Grief

The way in which you react to your loss.

- Grief has a wide range of feelings and emotions.
- While grief is usually manifested emotionally, it can also be expressed physically, spiritually, socially, and cognitively.
- Each person will express their grief in their own unique way.

Bereavement

The intense feelings you have after a loss due to death.

Bereavement can be the most uncomfortable time for you, as you are immersed in your grief and tend to feel your pain and sadness more deeply.

- The intense feelings in bereavement interfere with day-to-day functioning. Adults and children may:
- Be in shock and disbelief during this time.
- Feel overwhelmed.
- Be disorganized.
- Have difficulty concentrating.
- Have trouble sleeping, eating, working, paying attention in school.

Mourning

The way in which you process your grief and loss.

- Our culture may have the expectation that we are in mourning for a year, and then our loss or grief should be complete, which is incorrect.
- Mourning can last several months or several years.
- Families may mourn according to their religious or spiritual beliefs and practices.
- Various cultures experience mourning differently.

Different Ways Deaths Occur and How it Impacts Your Grieving Process

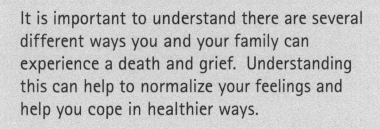

It is important to understand there are several different ways you and your family can experience a death and grief. Understanding this can help to normalize your feelings and help you cope in healthier ways.

Sudden Loss

This type of loss comes out of the blue and is totally unexpected.

- It often happens immediately and quickly.
- The response to this loss is often denial, shock, disbelief, and overwhelming feelings.
- This loss is more difficult to process, as there was no time for closure—to say goodbye.
- You can be left with lingering feelings of being robbed, cheated, or just plain angry.

Uncertain Loss

This type of loss creates a sort of limbo where you are uncertain if the person will live or die. For example, if a person is in a coma or sick.

- You don't know how long the person will be in this uncertain situation.
- You experience a great deal of ambiguity and stress.
- You can feel helpless and hopeless.
- You have trouble managing your emotions, or managing your emotions becomes very difficult.

Certain Loss

This is a loss that is expected and inevitable.

- You do have time to for closure and can say goodbye.
- You have a chance to process your grief and work through anything that is unfinished.
- Depending on where children are developmentally, they may or may not be able to process this loss, even though there is usually ample time to say goodbye.

Traumatic Loss

This is probably the most difficult to cope with because the loss is sudden and traumatic, such as a suicide, homicide, or catastrophic event.

- You don't have time for closure or to be able to say goodbye.
- This type of loss may lead to disenfranchised grief. Disenfranchised grief is a type of grief that is often not recognized or accepted by the culture.
- This loss can cause you to feel shame, embarrassment, confusion, and disbelief.
- These losses may lead to traumatic reaction in both children and adults.

Ways to Look at Grief

There has been much written about how to cope with the death of a person, whether or not you were close or not close to the person. Grief can be experienced in either situation. We wanted to provide you with theories that will offer helpful information and better clarify your understanding of your own grief journey.

 We want to provide you with helpful information to better clarify your understanding of your own grief journey.

Stages of Grieving

Dr. Elizabeth Kubler Ross, in 1969 worked for years with dying patients. She developed the Five Stages of Grieving. These stages have been widely accepted for almost four decades. It is important to point out that these stages were for the dying not the bereaved. New research in the field of bereavement has found that people may experience some of these stages not necessarily as stages, but more as experiences and not in any particular order.

Shock and Denial

You may also feel confusion, fear, and avoidance. You can't believe the person died.

Anger

You may feel anger or even rage along with frustration, impatience, irritation, and anxiety. You may feel anger in general or toward the person who died, or the toward the universe.

Bargaining

This stage is more related to people that are dying. However bereaved people who had a family member die from a long illness may experience this stage.

Depression

You may feel hopeless and helpless, at times even numb.

Acceptance

You begin to make peace with your situation.

♥ The death of a family member is undoubtedly one of the most traumatic kinds of losses. It takes enormous courage to face your pain, to sit with your discomfort, to feel your anguish.

"Hug a tree" activity during Kate's Club Memory Walk

Tasks of Mourning

At Kate's Club, we frame much of the work we do around the "Tasks of Mourning," created by William Worden. He believed that grief is not a passive progression of stages, but rather an active process. These tasks are fluid and nonlinear, and people may go back and forth between them. The following are the tasks of mourning.

Accept the reality of the loss by confronting denial. Accept the weight of the loss.

- For children, this means having age-appropriate explanations of death.

Experience the pain of grief.

- As a culture, we try to avoid pain at all costs. However, avoidance compounds our pain.
- Allow the emotions. Reach out to a trusted friend, clergy, or counselor to help you process the pain.
- Express your emotions creatively. Using art, journaling, or music may help if you have trouble talking about feelings.

Adjust to the world without the deceased.

- This may be the most difficult of the tasks.
- This is when you learn to live with the new normal.
- You might feel guilty as you learn to live and enjoy life again without the deceased as if you are betraying the person who died. It takes time to work through these feelings.

Find an enduring connection with the deceased while embarking on a new life.

- Much of our work at Kate's Club centers on helping children/teens and families stay connected to the person who died as they move forward.
- Think of all the ways the deceased shaped your life while discovering the next for yourself and your family.

Healthy Grief

The death of a family member is undoubtedly one of the most traumatic kinds of losses. It takes enormous courage to face your pain, to sit with your discomfort, to feel your anguish. Healthy grieving requires openness, awareness, and willingness to ask for help and support from others. Grieving together, with family or others, can help you move through the grieving process with a little more ease. Most children, teens, and adults, with time and support, will experience healthy grieving. Healthy grieving requires:

- A willingness to fully experience and express all your emotions.

- Recognizing your attachment to the person who died and honoring your relationship.

- Finding ways to reconcile the loss and reinvest in a new way of living your life.

Problematic Grief Reactions

There will be some who require extra support and professional help during their grief journey. As we have previously stated, our society still holds unrealistic expectations about how long and what should be expected when children/teens or adults grieve. These unrealistic expectations, along with lack of support, or in addition to prior and secondary losses, can potentially create unhealthy grief reactions. If you identify and understand these, you or your family members can seek out professional help and support.

As we start to examine each of these, it must be said that all grief is complex because people and relationships are complicated. When relationships are ended by a death, these complicated and complex grief situations are intensified. They tend to last much longer than what is generally experienced as more healthy grief reactions.

The following below are grief reactions that can interfere with your day-to-day life in a myriad of ways, making your ability to cope more difficult.

 Grief reactions that can interfere with your day-to-day life, making your ability to cope difficult.

Absent grief

This is the most extreme form of unexpressed grief. It can wreak havoc on you physically and emotionally. To have no reaction at all, weeks or months later, can be a sign that you need help expressing your feelings.

Disenfranchised grief

This type of grief, for example from a suicide, is generally shunned by society, which makes it much more difficult to acknowledge and process. It could also involve a relationship that is not recognized as "worthy" of grief, such as a divorced spouse or an estranged relationship with a parent.

Idealized grief

The person who died or the relationship with the person is placed on a pedestal. You forget the things that irritated or annoyed you about the person. With this type of grief, you focus only on the positive. If you have experienced the death of a spouse or partner, this may hinder you from attaching to others and eventually finding a new relationship. Bereaved parents may idealize their deceased child to the extent that they struggle with staying connected to child(ren) who are still alive, which may leave surviving child(ren) feeling unworthy or guilty.

Somatic grief

Your grief turns into real physical illness, or you experience physical symptoms in your body.

Delayed grief

You push aside your grief and your feelings at the critical stages of mourning. Sometimes you feel you need to delay your grief to maintain functioning or because you are having to help your children/teens cope with their grief and loss.

Complicated grief

Normal grief that becomes stuck and worsens over time. With this type of grief reaction, you have a hard time focusing, functioning and feel disorganized. It is not unusual for you to feel extremely sad and overwhelmed.

Family Healing

The death of a family member can radically shift the dynamics and roles in the family and disrupt family stability. It is important to understand the roles each family member played within the family and the individual relationships with the person who died.

Families are capable of being resilient after a significant loss. Consider which ways you can receive support. We hope that in the guidance we provide in this book, and in the support, you can receive from Kate's Club or a similar organization, your family will cultivate resilience as you journey through your own unique grieving process.

Your ability to successfully cope depends on the following:

- Stability of your family before the death
- Family roles and relationships before the death
- Support outside of the family (friends, professionals, neighbors)
- Support within the family (siblings, aunts, uncles, brother, and sister-in-law's etc.)
- Cultural practices

- Religious practices
- Financial resources
- Additionally, communication plays a vital role in how your family adapts.

Below are some positive ways to communicate within your family. Suggestions:

- Build in specific time to share your grief feelings as a family.
- Make sure your children/teen know they need to grieve their own way, and you will need to do the same.
- Let your teens and children know that there will be an adult(s) who will be available to them to just listen. It's important to let them know who that adult(s) is/are. Realize it is not just you!
- Let your friends and family know how to best support you. (They really don't know what you need.)
- Let your children and teens know that you cannot replace the parent who died.
- Remind your teen or child that he/she can't take the place of the deceased spouse, or sibling.
- As hard as it might be, let your children/teens know they can still be involved with your deceased ex-spouse's family if appropriate.

Circle of Support

Different people and organizations provide unique kinds of help. Think about creating a "circle of support." Below are some examples of people and organizations that can be a part of your circle of support.

- Your place of worship or certain people within your place of worship who can provide a listening ear.
- A few of your close friends and family who are good listeners.

- A few friends who you can have some fun with, or you could just be with and not talk about the death or loss.

- Your child(ren)'s school counselor.

- Your physician and your children/teens physician so that they can be supportive or make referrals if needed.

- Kate's Club, or a similar organization for your children/ teens and for you, too.

- Grief groups in your community or online groups.

- Your child(ren)'s supportive teachers with whom your children/teens may have a good relationship.

- Boys Scouts/Girl Scouts.

- Big Brother/Big Sister organizations.

- Supportive coaches and instructors.

Reflections

After thinking about your circle of support, consider writing down some of the people and organizations that can offer you and your family support.

....

....

....

....

....

....

....

....

....

....

....

Chapter Two

Talking to Children and Teens About Grief and Loss

"Anything that's human is mentionable, and anything that is mentionable can be more manageable. When we can talk about our feelings, they become less overwhelming, less upsetting, and less scary. The people we trust with that important talk can help us know that we are not alone."

–Fred Rogers

Developmental Responses to Death

Children and teens grieve, and it is essential for their healing. However, children and teens are unique in the way they grieve due to their age, their development, their life experiences, and how those around them model their grief. Most professionals in the field of bereavement and grief would agree that it's important to pay close attention to how your children and teens express their grief. Most importantly, they will all express themselves differently based where they are developmentally.

It is imperative that adults show as much compassion as possible and not be afraid of their children and teens' pain and emotions. Teens and children need adults to help them navigate the often confusing, painful, and emotional journey of grieving. This takes courage and patience. Their ability to ultimately heal will be the gift you give to them, and they in turn give to you.

In the section below, we will detail the different developmental stages and understanding of death.

Birth–18 Months:
- Disturbed sleeping patterns.
- Eating changes.
- Clinging to the caretaker.
- Lethargy.

18 Months–2 years:
- Fears of losing primary caretaker's love.
- Can't cope well with multiple changes.
- Keenly aware of nonverbal responses.
- Begin to realize they are missing someone in their family.
- Unable to verbalize feelings; therefore, they act them out in misbehavior.
- Clingy—demands for affection and approval.

- May regress to previous behaviors—bedwetting, thumb-sucking, etc.
- Daily asking for person who is not present.

3–6 years:
- Understands death as temporary
- Acts out feelings or act as if nothing has changed.
- Blames self; views death as being punished for being naughty.
- Maintains fantasies of their loved one's return.
- Fears abandonment.
- May be irritable and/or show aggression.

7–10 years:
- Preoccupied with death.
- Prevailing sadness, increased crying, or withdrawal.
- Fears the future, concerns about money, food, shelter, etc.
- Self-conscious about the family being different.
- Experiences conflict with friends.

> Grieving takes courage and patience. Children and teens ability to ultimately heal will be the gift you as a parent give to them, and they in turn give to you.

11–13 years:
- Understands the concept of death.
- Believes that death is irreversible.
- Anger can cover emotional pain.
- May withdraw from friends and activities and appear seem indifferent.

- May feel shame that their family is different or changed.
- Busy themselves with activities and friends seeking approval.
- May suffer a loss of identity and low self-esteem.

14–20 years:

- Overwhelmed with additional responsibility. Need to be careful to avoid setting up a parentified situation with the teen or young adult.
- Frequent mood swings.
- Outward denial of inner turmoil.
- Dependent/independent conflicts.
- Seeks peer approval; prefers friends over family.
- Wants to compensate feelings of loss with more possessions.
- Fears parental illness.
- Tests limits.
- Sensitive to family tensions.

WE ALL CAME FROM DIFFERENT PLACES, BUT WE'RE ALL COMING FROM THE SAME PLACE.

Kate's Club teens support one another

How to Talk to Children about Death

Young and Middle Age Children

- It's important to remember that young children may need to be educated about death.

- Use open and honest conversation along with age-appropriate language when talking to children.

- Even if they do not outwardly show it, they are experiencing grief. Some children do not show a reaction until a year or even two years after a death.

- Grief reactions often come out in children's behavior. (See developmental response to grief.)

- For young children, you may see their grief and desire to understand what happened come out in their play. Do not surprised to see them play "funeral" or even to draw disturbing pictures.

- Keep your explanations simple and let them lead the way with their natural curiosity.

- They will ask you questions. Answer them according to what they can developmentally understand.

- In the case of a long illness, many parents think it's best not to share how their loved one is doing. Yet professionals who work with children and death say it's important to keep children apprised of the situation as you go along. Do not assume children understand what is happening around them.

- After a death, take them to a quiet comforting place and talk with them in very concrete terms.

  - For example, "Your daddy's heart was not well. He had something called a heart attack. We did not know his heart was sick. He died, which means his body stopped working. This means he will not come back. He is not hungry, lonely, scared, or in pain."

- You may want to impart your spiritual beliefs, but remember, this may confuse children and lead to questions of visiting the deceased in heaven.
  - Young children take what you say very literally.
  - Some children may think if they try to harm themselves, they too can go to heaven to see their loved one.
- Let them know you will do your best to answer all their questions.
  - However, they also need to know you might not have all the answers.
- School-aged children may have a lot of interest in the biology of the death and ask questions about what happens after a death.
- Reassure children that the death was not their fault even if they do not ask. Remember, children tend to be egocentric, so when something bad happens, they may blame themselves.
- They may still ask repeatedly when the person will return as they still see death as reversible.
  - Be patient, which can be hard at times.
  - Answer their questions as straightforwardly as possible.
- Even though older children and teens may understand death more than younger children, they still may have a lot of questions.
- Again, be honest and answer questions, even if they make you uncomfortable. There are ways to explain even the hardest subjects in age-appropriate ways. We may say, "Mommy feels uncomfortable talking about this, but it is important for me to be honest with you."
- Keep lines of communication open. Talk frequently and casually about the person who died.

- You can share memories as things come to mind. These will help older children see that they can still stay connected with the person.
- Remind them that though a person is not here physically with us, we can stay connected to them.
- Remember, children are unique, and their grief reactions will be unique as well. Some may act if nothing has happened. Others will be visibly upset and show their emotions.

> Remember, children are unique, and their grief reactions will be unique as well.

Simple Reminders When Talking with Teens

- Be respectful of your teen's grief process
- Be an observer
- Welcome their feelings
- Talk openly and honestly about the death
- Avoid euphemisms
- Share your feelings
- Include them in funerals and other ceremonies
- Though it is fine and even healthy for teens to take on more responsibilities, it is important not to overburden them. Remind them they are still children and you are a parent. For example, no teen should be expected to be the man of the house.

Sibling Loss

"When a brother or sister dies, the children left behind are mourning not only the loss of that sibling, but also the loss of the shape of the family."

-Ann Farrat

The death of a sibling is perhaps one of the most neglected types of grief. Many times, emphasis is put on the parents, and the child or teen may be asked, "How are your parents?" They may be told, "Oh, your poor parents! You must be strong for them." However, siblings share a unique bond that may shift and change over the course of time. They may be best playmates and/or rivals. They may swing between love, jealousy, and caring for a younger sibling. Attention needs to be paid to the unique pain caused by the death of a sibling.

In addition to the grief reactions mentioned earlier, there are some related specifically to sibling loss.

Reactions and concerns around sibling loss

- Shift in roles within family
- Sometimes amplification of distinguishing role: the good girl vs. the rebel
- Triggers at milestones and events
- Feelings of increased responsibility many times related to protecting parents
- Regret of past with sibling—regret being jealous of sibling
- Survivor's guilt—may feel like the wrong sibling died
- Family may idealize child who died
- Experience second loss if parent(s) ability to parent is compromised

Tips for your family:

- Get your own help so you can be there for your children. We hear from adults who experienced the death of a sibling when they were a child that they wish their parents had gotten help with their own grief. Reach out to a therapist that specializes in child loss and you may find a group of other bereaved parents will help.

- Talk about your child who died authentically. Try not to idealize but share all the memories good and not so good. Your surviving child(ren) will be less likely to compare themselves in a negative light.

- Spend time together and nurture each individual relationship in your family.

- Check in with child(ren) and allow them to express their feelings without protecting you. Ensure them that you will be okay.

- Realize how milestones and ages may affect your children.

- Get support for whole family. You may wish to do some family counseling or take part in family groups for sibling loss.

Kate's Club activities allow families to share their memories

Helping Children and Teens Cope with Suicide, Homicide, and Overdose Deaths

In chapter one, we defined the different types of grief. In this section, we will go into more detail about how to support your children and teens when they are faced with a more traumatic or stigmatized death. Please note, generally children under the age of three or four are not able to understand the complexity of these type of grief reactions. Refer to the section on developmental understanding of grief.

Suicide

The suicide of a friend or loved one is a devastating experience. Suicide survivors are often left with many painful questions and emotions. Suicide is very hard to understand and make sense out of, even for many adults. This loss can lead to disenfranchised grief for children/teens and adults. Thus, it is understandable to be overwhelmed or unsure of how to explain suicide to children.

Tips for Children:

- Simple, truthful information about what has occurred is very important to express to them.
- Encourage them to ask questions about the suicide at their own pace.
- Show love, support, and reassurance.
- Children need to know that often if a person dies by suicide, they have a mental illness. Talking about this can help increase understanding.

 Children and teens can react with great confusion, sadness, anger and a sense of guilt.

- Let children know that many people who die of suicide struggle with a mental illness called depression.

- Depression can be explained to children as when a person feels very, very sad and doesn't feel that there is anything they can do to make life better, so they do something to harm or kill themselves.

  - You may say, "Mommy had a disease called depression, and it made her very sad. Most of the time people with depression do not kill themselves, but sometimes they do. However, there is always another choice."

- IMPORTANT: Children need to know that they are not responsible for the death, and nothing they said or did could have stopped it.

- Sometimes people who die of suicide do so because they feel that their friends and loved ones would be better off without them.

Reactions in Children after a Death by Suicide

- Shame
- Guilt
- Anger
- Confusion

Teens and Suicide Loss

It's important to point out that for teens, a parent suicide can be extra traumatic because of this turbulent developmental stage. They are struggling with trying to separate themselves from their parents and at the same time may be very comforted by knowing there is an adult available to them. When a parent dies by suicide, this can wreak havoc with their already complicated relationships with their parents.

If a teen loses a peer or sibling to suicide, there can be great confusion, sadness, and a sense of guilt.

- Patience, patience, and more patience! Teens tend to be very moody during this time and can flip back and forth from trying to be very adultlike and shifting back into more childish behavior.

- Teens can have very intense feelings around complicated grief situations, so give them time and space to work some of it out. It may need to be with another adult or professional.

- They may try to comfort themselves with alcohol or drugs.

- Sometimes recommending a physical outlet can be comforting and help release some of their intense feelings.

- Peer groups specific to suicide can be very helpful to adults and teens.

- Children who have had a parent die from suicide are at a higher risk to die by suicide someday. The more you can keep an open dialogue about mental health, the better chance you have to prevent this from happening.

Homicide

Unfortunately, children and teens are exposed to quite a lot of simulated violent deaths on video games, the internet, TV, and even real ones in their own families. When children or teens are personally impacted by a sudden, traumatic death from a homicide, it is not unusual for them to experience complicated, unnatural, and overwhelming grief. To top it off, how the person died and whether they were present can be extremely painful and difficult to process. Additionally, there can be much shame along with a sense of numbness.

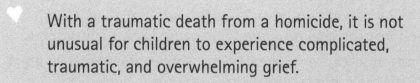

With a traumatic death from a homicide, it is not unusual for children to experience complicated, traumatic, and overwhelming grief.

They will need your support, some adult close to them, and/or professional support, for many months or years after. As has been mentioned, this is a disenfranchised grief.

- Don't overwhelm children with too much information, and don't try to hide the truth from them. Share information in age-appropriate ways.

- Monitor and respond to any questions the child asks.

- Provide comfort, security, and reassurance.

  - For example, "It is my job as your mommy to do everything I can to keep you safe."

- Provide structure and routine to decrease feelings of chaos in their world.

- Example: For a young child you might say: "A sad, terrible thing has happened that is not your fault. Daddy was walking to his car and a bad man shot him with a gun. Daddy was hurt very badly, and he died."

- Limit news and social media exposure.

Common Reactions of Children After a Death by Homicide

- Shock/Disbelief
- Fear/Terror
- Guilt
- Confusion
- Shame
- Anger
- Loss of sense of safety and order in their world
- Significant grief

Overdose Deaths/Long-term Substance Abuse

Many but not all people who die from drug-related deaths have struggled with addiction. If a person has struggled before an overdose death or if the person dies from conditions related to their addiction, the following can be helpful in explaining addiction.

Distinguish between drugs of abuse and medicine used properly prescribed by a doctor. You might say, "Addiction is a disease that causes a person to use more alcohol and drugs than is safe. It can be treated, but it sometimes ends in death."

Talking with Children

- Before you talk with your children, consider their prior knowledge of the family member's substance use.

  - They might realize that person had problems, and/or they may have been exposed to upheaval and change caused by the addiction.

  - Other children may not be aware that their family member struggled with drug-related issues.

  - Either way, it can be difficult for children to understand.

- Ground yourself before speaking with a child. Choose a calm and private place.

- Share (with children who are developmentally more able to process information), that addiction can control the brain and cause the person to do or say hurtful things that they do not really mean.

- Tell the truth in an age-appropriate way. You can add more information over time as the child can understand and process in a more mature way.

- Resist the urge to vilify the person who died. If the child thinks, "Daddy was weak and bad," then the child may also think, "Maybe I am, too."

  - The way a person dies should not define their whole life.

- You can start with asking the child what they know and what they think about the death. This will give you a starting point for the conversation.

- Children sense when they are not told the truth. They may also hear it from others. This can lead to feelings of betrayal and distrust. It is best they hear it in the beginning from a trusted adult.

- Explain overdose deaths truthfully in age-appropriate terms. You may say, "An overdose is when someone takes too much of the wrong drug or too much of a drug and their body stops working." It may be tempting to hide the truth or make up vague stories.

- Children may have many conflicting feelings about the person who died. Reassure them that it is okay to have all kinds of feelings. They may feel protective and loyal, but also feel disappointed, hurt, and/or angry.

Talking with Teens

- Teens need to know the truth, even if they don't want to hear it.

- Talk to teens about the predisposition in families related to addiction.

  - Talk openly and honestly so that they can use this information when making decisions about alcohol and drug use.

  - This can help them learn more about how to break the cycle of addiction.

- Teens may need to have another adult they trust to talk with instead of you. Or a professional counselor or teen therapy group could be indicated.

Reflections

♥ Do you openly talk to your child/teens about the death? If not, what ideas and information in this chapter might help you communicate with your child/teens?

Chapter Three

Taking Care of Yourself While Grieving and Parenting

"Grief is a personal journey, never the same for any two people and as unique as your life and your relationships."

-Jeffery Brantley, MD

Your Own Grief Matters

Many parents often express how hard it is to grieve, to find the time and space, particularly because of having to support their children and teens who are also grieving. "There's no time for me! I have to be strong for my children/teens. There is so much I have to do now." This is a commonly shared sentiment, yet it is critical that you acknowledge and carve out time to process your grief. Your own grief matters. As we state throughout this book, healing requires allowing yourself to process your emotions.

Finding Time for Your Own Grief

The grieving process can catch you off guard or throw you off balance. Anyone who has experienced the death of someone close knows that "grief comes in waves." One day, you may feel anxious, angry, and very sad, and the next day, feel some relief or a little less sad. Then, the day after, back to sadness and feeling anxious and overwhelmed. Through these ups and downs, you try to hold yourself together so that you can parent your children, eventually go back to work if you were working, and somehow keep up with all the routine tasks, in addition to new ones. This feels daunting and draining, and it can leave you feeling like you are going crazy. You may wonder, "How will I stay sane while grieving and parenting?" This chapter focuses on information and ideas on how to honor your feelings, give yourself permission to take the time to grieve, and remind yourself of the importance of self-care.

Beliefs You May Hold

Finding time for your own grief, can get sidetracked by some of the beliefs you may hold. These beliefs can become excuses for not making time to process your own grief. Below are some examples of beliefs, see if any sound familiar to you.

- You feel, as the surviving parent, that you must be a positive role model for your children/teens, and you think that they should see you are strong, which for you means they shouldn't see you grieving.

- You believe you must be completely available to your children and teens and try to be super mom or dad, so push aside your own grief.

- You believe you have to support your spouse or partner if you have experienced the death of a child.

- You feel pressure from others that you must be strong, which reinforces that you cannot break down.

- You feel you are being selfish if you allow yourself time to grieve.

- You push your grief aside so that you have the energy needed to do the things you must do.

- It's too painful to acknowledge your grief. You are afraid of acknowledging your feelings, as you might lose control and embarrass yourself.

"Warrior Moms" - A Group for bereaved mothers

Unrealistic and Realistic Expectations

Unrealistic expectations get in the way of your grieving process. Unrealistic expectations are the beliefs that are not practical, feasible, or achievable. These beliefs are often accompanied by statements you tell yourself such as, "I should," "I must," or "I ought to." What we have learned from many of the parents at Kate's Club is that it's hard to let go of some of these unrealistic expectations. The following are some ideas to consider:

Letting Go of Unrealistic Expectations

Are you willing to:

- Recognize what you can and can't do and acknowledge your own limitations.

- Learn to say "no" to expectations both from others and yourself. (Frequently we say yes when we really mean no.)

- Let go of the things you can't control.

- Ask for support and help and be clear about what you need. For example, "Can you pick up Jordan from school tomorrow?"

- Recognize that by letting yourself grieve, you are modeling healthy grieving for your children.

Kate's Club family activity "Broken Pot"

Taking the Time for You

Many parents at Kate's Club talk about not having enough time for themselves. Your life has changed significantly. Yet we also know that if you don't take time for you, your ability to heal and support your children will be impacted. We believe this is a topic that needs special attention. Consider asking yourself the following questions.

- Do I really have to do all of this by myself?

- Can I really do all this without jeopardizing my own health and well-being? So often Kate's Club parents share they feel it is their job or responsibility. "No one can do this except me!" Is that really true?

- Do I feel, "I should," "I must," or "I ought to" do everything on my list? If you answer yes, then most likely you are not committed to taking time for you.

There are ways to build in some self-care time, but you need to be creative. Below are a few suggestions:

- Perhaps, when you drop your children off for carpool, you use some of that time for self-care time, instead of immediately running errands or texting or returning calls?

    - If you have errands that need to be done, prioritize them.

    - Think about whether someone else could do one or two of them for you.

    - Let your friends/family know that you might not always respond to their texts or phone calls in as timely a manner as they would expect, and tell them why.

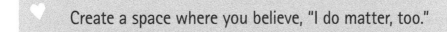

Create a space where you believe, "I do matter, too."

- Set aside a certain amount of time in your day and let your children/teens know that time that is your self-care time, just for you. Explain that there are to be no interruptions unless in an emergency. This may be the time when they can watch TV or play a video game.

- If your children are too young to understand what is meant by self-care time, or can't be left alone, then be intentional about taking time when they are sleeping or playing safely in their crib or playpen.

- For parents who are working, taking time for yourself is particularly important. Many Kate's Club parents are single parents. They have shared that they find this almost impossible. However, they also know they must do so for their own sanity, even if it's only a couple of times a week.

  - They share that it's when they don't build in some self-care time that they find they are the most impatient or angry with their children or themselves.

- Reach out to friends/neighbors and family and tell them you need some self-care time. Be specific about what they can do to support you.

  - Would they commit to a certain amount of time to watch your child(ren) on a regular basis?

  - Would they run some errands for you?

  - Would they be willing to commit to making one meal a week for you?

  - Would they help with some of the yard work?

Self-Care is Self-Compassion

After a death, you may not think about self-compassion. Self-compassion requires learning how to become "self-full." Becoming self-full involves being able to set boundaries and limits, learning to say no (without feeling guilty), and not allowing yourself to get caught up in beliefs that keep you from taking care of yourself. Self-compassion means taking care of yourself physically, emotionally, and spiritually. A self-full person takes into consideration other people's feelings and needs, but not at the expense of themselves. Lastly, being self-full takes courage and then a willingness to being open to other options, to let go of beliefs that don't serve you well, to ask for help, and then to allow others to help you as best as they can.

Rest and sleep.

- Rest and sleep are essential to good self-care. They restore the mind, body, and spirit.

- Grieving adults report they have trouble sleeping after the death of a loved one and so need to be mindful of getting a good night's sleep

- If your child(ren) sleep in your bed, a good night's sleep may be difficult. When it comes to be an issue, work on getting them back in their beds.

- Try to get in a bedtime routine that relaxes you. Avoid reading your phone or computer at least 30 minutes before bed. Try a light- hearted TV show or read a book.

- Try a nighttime tea like chamomile.

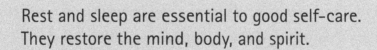

♥ Rest and sleep are essential to good self-care. They restore the mind, body, and spirit.

Being mindful of your body.

- Your body is not able to take care of itself without some love and attention. Think about how you show self-compassion to your body. It's important to check in with your body every so often.

  - Is your body well-nourished with food and hydration?

- Do you listen to what your body is telling you? Your body talks to you through physical expression (pain, palpitations, soreness, stiffness, sluggishness, headaches, backaches, gaining or losing weight, or exhaustion).

- Make sure you get your routine physicals.

- Give your body a gift, such as a massage, a nice long soak in a tub, or a yoga session.

- Take some time for exercise. Walk or do another exercise while your children are at sports practice. Go for family walks or bike rides.

Comforting Yourself

While it's wonderful to receive comfort from others, it's also very important to learn how to provide comfort to yourself. Think about what your positive comforts might be and be aware of how you may use negative comforts.

Positive comforts might include
- Spending time with friends who fill your spirit
- Gardening or sitting in your garden
- Finding a peaceful space to pray or just have quiet time
- Participating in an exercise routine that makes you feel good

Negative comforts might involve
- Keeping yourself so busy you have no time to recognize how you are truly feeling
- Indulging in too much alcohol, food, or other addictive behaviors

Mindfulness
Pay attention to how you feel in the present moment and do so in a nonjudgmental way. It requires that you slow down

and connect to your heart so that you can fully experience yourself and the life around you.

Mindfulness embraces the qualities of compassion, patience, and kindness. It can bring more balance and ease into your life.

Breath and Breathing

We take breathing for granted. We often fail to recognize how powerfully healing breathing can be.

Paying attention to your breathing, particularly when grieving, can help ground you, calm you, and release some of the sadness and stress you are feeling.

Below is a simple breathing meditation you can do perhaps when you wake up and before you go to sleep and of course any time during the day when you are feeling overwhelmed.

- I breathe in compassion and exhale fear
- I breathe in kindness and exhale anger
- I breathe in joy and exhale sadness
- I breathe in ease and exhale discomfort

Meditation

There are many ways to approach meditation. There are more formal meditation practices such as Buddhist and Zen practices, and informal, mindfulness-based meditation.

We suggest you find a way that feels most comfortable for you. You don't have to sit in a particular position or pose or even be in a specific setting. It can be practiced at home, work, in your garden or even in your car! Popular meditation apps include Calm and Headspace.

- Meditation teaches you to quiet your mind and body so your whole being can be at rest.
- It helps you connect to your body by listening to your breathing and heartbeat.
- And it helps you to slow down and calm your spirit.

Non-traditional Meditation

There are other ways to engage in meditation that will clear your mind, so you can release your stress and worries for a little while.

Slowly build in quiet time. You may need to start with just 5 minutes a couple of times and day and then build up to 20 to 30 minutes if possible.

 Think of activities that calm and relax you and clear your "monkey mind."

Teach your children about the importance of their own quiet time. Perhaps set up family quiet time. Think of activities that calm and relax you and clear your "monkey mind." (The mental chatter that feeds your stress and overwhelm.)

Consider

- Listening to music
- Gardening
- Swimming
- Hiking
- Cooking
- Singing
- Reading a good novel
- Dancing
- Sewing
- Arts and crafts, drawing, painting, or even using an adult coloring book
- Golfing and fishing

Humor and Laughter

After the death of a loved one, it may seem impossible to consider that you can and will be able to laugh again. It feels so incongruent to the pain and sadness you feel. Yet, a good laugh can bring endorphins into your body and make you feel better.

- You may feel guilty when you find yourself laughing. Yet part of healing is to recognize that you don't have to live in your pain and sadness all day and every day.

- Remembering some of the funny things that the person who died did or said may start to relieve some of the sadness.

- Laughter and humor produce endorphins and are great antidepressants. In other words, laughter and humor are healthy and are important ways to help you heal.

- You might find ways to laugh at things in the grieving process and sometimes even find "dark humor." You may not expect to hear laughter at a grief group, but at Kate's Club, there is a lot of laughter as people share their stories.

Loneliness

Loneliness plays a huge part in loss. Your loneliness can be so profound that it overtakes your grief. You may try to distract yourself by staying busy. Keeping busy is a common antidote to loneliness. However, once you sit still for a moment or get ready to go to sleep at night, loneliness creeps in. It can be overpowering. As one spouse shared (which many spouses/ex-spouses have echoed), "Loneliness can take on a life of its own; it deadens all my other feelings." Without your loved one, you may feel lonely even when you are around other people. You may feel lonely even though you are rarely alone, which is the case with most single parents.

There are ways to cope with loneliness, and the following are some suggestions:

Acknowledge, "I am lonely." Then sit with it. Don't judge it or try to talk yourself out of being lonely.

Observe. You may feel lonely.

 Loneliness will not always be your constant companion.

Give yourself permission to be lonely. There will be times when you are lonely. Activities and people will come into your life to offset some of the loneliness.

- Think about the good listeners and comforting people in your life. Ask them to check in with you for a while.

- Make one plan a day to do something for yourself that helps you feel connected to other people or activities.

- Find one activity that you can participate in on a regular basis that nurtures and fills your spirit.

- Connect to others who have had a spouse/partner or child die. Consider finding a support group.

- Recognize there will be times when you crave physical touch and closeness of the person who died, particularly if this was your spouse or partner. While it is no substitute, you can give yourself the gift of a massage and ask people you are close with for a hug.

- Hugging your children or your pets can provide a different but important type of touch and physical closeness as well.

- Realize that the holidays, celebrations such as birthdays, anniversaries, or special places, can underscore your loneliness. Plan how you will spend those days and with whom.

Learning to Love Again: Dating After Losing a Spouse

This is a topic that brings so many mixed feelings: From, "Are you kidding me? Never again." To, "I feel so lonely that I do hope to find someone to love again." The idea of getting out in the dating world is overwhelming and frightening. Thinking about falling in love and possibly losing again, intolerable!

Many of our Kate's Club parents share that they get so much advice from friends, families, and work colleagues about dating. While they all are coming from a place of love and caring, sometimes the advice they give you often makes you feel more confused and angrier. You may want to think about the following as you decide whether or not to date again.

Consider

The type of relationship you had with your spouse or ex-spouse.

- How long were you together?

- How did your spouse die? That can impact how you grieve. For example, if your spouse was sick for a long time, you may have done some anticipatory grieving. If it was a sudden death, you will most likely be in shock or even denial, and it might take time to allow yourself to grieve.

- Did you have a close relationship, or were you having marital issues, separated, or divorced?

- Will unfinished business (the things you never resolved) impact the decisions and choices you make going forward?

You know intellectually you cannot replace your spouse with someone else, but your heart may try to compare/contrast the new person you begin to date.

Ask yourself

- Am I able to move aside my grief and feelings enough, so I can go into a new relationship open-minded and openhearted?

- How do I handle my guilt about wanting to date again, especially when I so loved my deceased spouse?

- Am I dating to keep from feeling sad and lonely? In other words, am I using dating to put a Band-Aid on my grief?

- Am I dating because I feel bad about myself? Some people do not like to think of themselves as single and have been a part of a couple for a long time. They feel less than when not in a relationship.

- Am I ready to open myself sexually? Will I expect to have similar feelings with someone new as I had with my spouse?

- Do I want to meet someone like my spouse or someone very different?

- How will I handle rejection? Getting out there brings the natural risk of rejection. Grieving can make you feel extra vulnerable and less able to handle rejection.

- Dealing with friends and family around dating can sometimes be very challenging. Some may insist that it's been long enough and that you should start dating, while others feel that you have not waited long enough.

- What do I say to them if I don't want to date? How do I handle their often well-intentioned but critical advice or commentary?

- How do I navigate the topic of dating with the kids?
  - Figure out if you want to talk to your children about dating again or keep it quiet for a while. Younger children especially may want you to date to meet a new mom or dad.
  - You may not want to tell your children right away when you start to date. Instead, introduce the subject slowly.

- Consider getting to know someone well before introducing them to your children
- How do I know when it is time to start dating again?
- How do I even start dating?
  - Do I go to online dating sites?
  - Do I tell my friends to set me up?
  - Do I go to bars or parties to try to meet someone?
  - Where are there safe places to meet someone?

Tips

- First, take time to figure out who you are now. Whether you like it or not, you are not the same person you were with your spouse. Likely, this grief experience has changed you in many ways.
- Journaling might also help you get more clarity. Write about your hopes for the future and what kind of person you hope to meet.
- Be cautious of meeting someone in hopes they will take your pain away.
- Be ready for potential rejection. That is hard if you are already feeling hurt and vulnerable. Reach a point where you feel confident in yourself.
- Try to meet new people. For example you might
  - Join a hiking group or tennis team.
  - Explore a new hobby.
  - Join a health club.
  - Take a class.
  - Join a book club.
  - Consider getting involved in your faith of worship.

- Keep in mind that most people have never dated a widower or widow, and they may not be used to someone speaking lovingly about someone they were married to.
  - Talking constantly about your spouse may be a sign you are not ready.
  - On the other hand, if you bring up your spouse occasionally and the person you are dating is kind and supportive, that is a good sign.
  - It is important to meet someone who understands that your grief is a journey, but you are ready to also move forward.

 Remember loving and grieving can happen at the same time.

Ex-Spouses and Ex-Partners

Many parents who bring their children to Kate's Club were no longer with the parent who has died. The ex-spouse or ex-partners may face their own complicated feelings and experience less support without a current spouse or partner.

Below are some scenarios that might be familiar to you.

- You may have had a difficult relationship with the deceased.
  - You might be angry because the person did not step up as a parent to your child(ren) or still be hurt and angry from experiences in your relationship.
  - Therefore, you may be processing your grief very differently than your child.

- You may be experiencing intense grief that you did not expect.
  - Many parents tell us that they experience unexpected grief feelings after losing their ex-spouse or partner.
  - You may miss the co-parent, friend, and grieve all the shared memories.
  - Others may not recognize your grief. The grief of an ex is sometimes called, "disenfranchised grief." (Disenfranchised grief is grief that is not socially recognized or supported.)
  - People think that since you are no longer together, especially if you were not on good terms, then you do not have the right to be sad.

Consider

- If your relationship was troubled, think about writing a letter to the deceased. Perhaps the reason your relationship was troubled was the person's inability to listen.
- Recognize that you have the right to grieve, and make room to process your grief.
- Reach out to supportive people in your life. Let others know when their comments and judgment are not helpful to you.
- You may need to explain to your current partner or spouse that you feel connected to the deceased based on the co-parenting relationship or prior relationship and that you feel grief that your child has lost a parent.
- You may feel the burden of losing your co-parent and must find new means of support. Perhaps, your ex took your child(ren) half the time and/or they helped in all parenting decisions. Let extended family members and friends know you may need extra help now.
- Even if parents were no longer together, children will most likely enjoy hearing stories and memories of their parents.
- Share positive memories and stories of the deceased with your children.

Non-Custodial Parents Becoming Full-Time Parents

- This will bring on huge changes for you, especially if you are used to a much smaller role.

- Be patient with yourself and your child. Your child(ren) may have had to leave their full-time home and change schools, and in some cases, move far from their other family friends.

- Look for support for your children in your area. Strive to help them become used to their new area.

- If they have a new room, help them fix it up. Let them decide what to keep from their former house. Know they may want to keep items of their deceased parent, and make room for those possessions.

- Ensure they feel comfortable putting pictures of the deceased up in their room if they wish to do so.

Parents and children support each other

Reflections

Think about a few ways you will commit to self-care and write them down.

Chapter Four

Grandparents Raising Grandchildren

"It takes patience because it is difficult to watch a child in pain without wanting to fix it or make it go away."

-Alan Wolfelt, Finding the Words

Grandparents Issues

At Kate's Club, we often see grandparents stepping into the role of parent. This chapter will offer advice for that situation and touch on grandparents' grief for their adult children and their grandchildren.

Many children at Kate's Club are being raised by grandparents. This usually happens when a child loses a parent and the other parent is not able, willing, or not suitable to raise the child. In some situations, grandparents raise children when both parents die. Most of the time, this means the grandparent grieves an adult child while raising a child. Whatever the case, it is most likely not a situation you planned for. Grandparents in all different circumstances may now find raising children to be quite different from when they raised their own children. These situations can come as a complete surprise and take some adjustments.

Below are common circumstances and ideas to cope with this new and challenging time.

Circumstances
- You may still be working and must navigate childcare again.
- You may be enjoying having an empty nest and now have children back in your nest.
- You may still be raising your own younger children and now must add your grandchildren to the mix.
- After many years of being in the grandparent role, you may find yourself back in the parent role.

Challenges
- Grandparents often share they miss being able to spoil their grandchild(ren) and having that special relationship as they now must become parents to their grandchildren. You may find yourself grieving the loss of the role of grandparent as well.

- As a grandparent, you may feel out of touch with schooling, trends, and other current parenting philosophies.

- You may feel out of place with your grandchildren's friends' parents.

- Your own friends may not desire to do things with younger children, so you may lose connections.

- You may face new financial strains, especially if you are on a fixed income, and you may have to move to accommodate your growing family.

- You may struggle to balance your feelings of grief while having to support your grandchildren's grief.

- You may be missing the life you planned for after your children grew up or in your retirement.

- You may be facing health issues, and/or you find you do not have the energy to keep up with younger children.

- You may be faced with being a caregiver to other family members such as elder parents while raising children.

Suggestions

- Ask for help and be specific! You will need to identify what you need and ask directly for help. Most people do want to help.

- Look for networks of other grandparents raising grandchildren. You may wish to join a program that helps link grandparents to resources and provides a social network.

- Address your own grief by finding a therapist and/or support group.

- Recognize this is a life-altering event, so be patient and gentle with yourself.

- Keep connected with other family members, as they can be of great help.

- Stay connected with friends who you know will be supportive and not continually offer advice. Update wills and guardianship documents.

- For help with custody concerns, look to local legal aid groups if needed.

- Practice your own self-care as addressed earlier in this book.

- Do your best to keep yourself healthy by keeping your medical appointments.

- Incorporate activities that can nurture you, such as Yoga, Pilates, Tai Chi, water aerobics, prayer, or reading the Bible or other spiritual books.

Grandmother who raised her grandson has a special bond

Reflections

♥ Think about little ways you can do something nice for yourself.

"Healing Heart" - A Kate's Club activity

Chapter Five

Resilience in Our Children and Teens: Kate's Club Kids Thrive

> "Resilience is our ability to bounce back from the stresses of life. It's not avoiding the stressor but learning to thrive within it."
>
> -The Other Side of Sadness, by George Bonanno

Defining Resilience

At Kate's Club, we believe very strongly that there are many ways to help children and teens build resilience. When thinking of children experiencing the death of a parent or sibling, our minds tend to go to more negative outcomes. No doubt, children and teens are at risk for depression, anxiety, lower, academic success, and lower levels of self-esteem and self-efficacy. Yet children and teens do not become resilient unless they face adverse circumstances. Since your children or teens are facing adversity, they now have a chance to build resilience.

 Resilience is something that can be learned over time, and you can help build it. At Kate's club we have seen some children and teens grow amazingly resilient!

Factors that Impact Resilience

- Cultivating at least one stable and committed relationship with a supportive parent, or another trusting adult.
- Acknowledging personality and temperament.
- Recognizing the environment that children/teens are living in.
- Finding extracurricular activities that provide positive ways for children and teens to engage with peers and adults.

Building Resilience in Your Children and Teens

The key ingredients to building resilience are support, encouragement, and knowledge. Evidence supports that having a peer role model, that is, knowing someone who has had a similar experience and who has experienced death, can facilitate growth. As an adult role model, you can also help facilitate support. Below are some ideas:

- Encourage positive social interactions with children and teens. If your child struggles with social skills, consider role-playing situations or even finding a social skills group.

- Develop a strong emotional connection between your child/teen and yourself.

- Seek out at least one caring non-parent adult in their lives, such as coaches, mentors, teachers, neighbors, and extended family members.

- Teach coping skills, particularly around how to handle hard emotions like anger, fear, and frustration.

- Provide outlets for expression through play, exercise, and the arts.

- Identify resources that can help your family. These can be financial, emotional, and spiritual. For example:
  - Connect with Kate's Club or a similar type of organization.
  - Consider counseling or other mental health services.
  - Reach out to your faith community or consider connecting with a local spiritual community.
  - Make sure you take advantage of all the financial resources that may be available to you such as:
    - Food stamps
    - Local food banks
    - Social security for your children
    - Housing assistance you might be able to access

Offer Encouragement for the Future

Children and teens need to know that things will change, that they won't always feel the way they feel right now. Remind them that they are resilient by:

- Sharing with them ways they have handled hardships in the past.

- Labeling their emotions and then normalizing them.

- Embracing mistakes, both yours and your children and teens.

- Finding ways to helping them become more self-aware, which can build self-efficacy, or confidence in their "ability to succeed in a particular situation."

- Consider utilizing the Nurtured Heart Approach to galvanize resilience (see below).

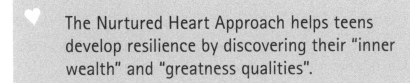

The Nurtured Heart Approach helps teens develop resilience by discovering their "inner wealth" and "greatness qualities".

The Nurtured Heart Approach (NHA): Helping Children and Teens Recognize Their Greatness Qualities

The Nurtured Heart Approach (NHA) is an innovative way to help children and teens develop resilience. They can become more self-aware, build self-efficacy, and develop what the NHA describes as "inner wealth." The main philosophy behind this approach created by Howie Glasser is to "mine out their greatness qualities." Most adults tend to point out, and therefore "energize" by their tone of voice and their words, what children and teens do wrong. The Nurtured Heart Approach requires focusing and energizing what your child is doing right! Using words that describe what they are doing right and how it shows their strength of character, going beyond "thank you" and "good job," is essential to building inner wealth. For example:

- If their job is to take out the garbage every week (even if they get paid for it), let them know you appreciate what they are doing and then describe in words why you appreciate what they are doing. You might start out by saying," Thank you for taking out the garbage." Then utilizing the NHA, use descriptive words by saying, "We appreciate your following through with this task, even though you don't like doing it. It shows you listen and are dependable."

- Or, if they are supposed to do their homework, for example, you could articulate their positive behavior by saying, "I see you are doing your homework first, instead of going out and playing. That shows you are making wise choices and are being responsible."

- Or, when they start playing together and are not quibbling with one another, let them know you noticed that they are being respectful or playing nicely with one another.

  You might say, "You two are playing nicely together! It shows me that you respect one another, even when at times you may want to yell at your sister or brother. That takes great patience and caring!"

This program has been around for twenty-plus years and has shown great success with difficult child and teen issues.

Friendship

It goes without saying that children and teens need peer interaction and support. It helps them learn, grow, and thrive. After a young person experiences the death of a parent, primary caregiver, or sibling, their world turns upside down. To make matters more challenging, many of their friends may not have ever experienced a death of someone close and do not know how to show support. Additionally, as we have mentioned previously, our society does a poor job of acknowledging death. And many people struggle talking about it with young people. Deaths by suicide or homicide may leave children and teens feeling especially isolated from friends.

At Kate's Club, we have learned from our children and teens that their peers sometimes make very unpleasant and at times mean comments to them. Sometimes, children are even bullied because of their loss. The following are a few examples they have shared with us:

- "Sorry about the death of your father, but at least you still have your mother."

- "Aren't you over your grief by now? It's been a few weeks."

- "Well, you told me you didn't like your mom, so you must be glad she died."

- "I would kill myself if you were my kid, too."

- " Now you don't have to worry about your father punishing you for stupid stuff."

It can be devastating for young people to hear those types of comments from a peer. They can leave an indelible mark on their heart. Unfortunately, adults, too, may make similar remarks, not realizing the implications.

Teens have shared how painful it can be to listen to their friends complain or make nasty comments about parents. Teens who have had a parent die may feel very sensitive to missing their own parent, yet not feel comfortable saying so to their friends.

At Kate's Club, we help children and teens learn how to handle unkind or inappropriate statements. Having the opportunity to share with others who understand provides tremendous relief. Teens especially bond over sharing insensitive comments they hear from people. It is so painful for them to process these statements on their own. Children and teens feel validated and powerful when someone listens and understands. The combination of peer and trained adult support can't be understated.

The following are suggestions on how to help children or teens handle difficult remarks:

- Gently encourage your child or teen to share what was said. Just listen.

- Then, ask how that remark made them feel. If they are having trouble expressing how they feel, perhaps share how it would make you feel.

- Acknowledge that the remarks made were inappropriate and unkind.

- Provide some different statements your child or teen can say when unkind or inappropriate remarks are said, such as:

  - What you said to me was hurtful and not helpful.

  - You don't know what I am going through. What you said is not my truth.

  - I need you to just listen, which is how you show me that you care.

  - What you said to me is not okay.

- Explain to your child or teen that most people who haven't experienced the death of a parent or sibling don't really understand and don't know what to say.

- Teens may have a harder time saying something back to their peers because they want to be accepted by their peers. You might have to explore their feelings in more depth, particularly how they want to approach their peers.

Helping Your Children/Teens Maintain Friendships

It's also important that you encourage your children
to maintain their friendships with those who haven't
experienced a death. Friendships are critical for children
and teens when there has been a death of a parent or sibling.
Friendships can endure during times of grief and can help
them stay grounded in the present and future.

- Children need the opportunity to have fun and play with
  other children. Play and distraction help to ease sadness and
  provide positive ways to help them cope. As we mentioned in
  chapter two, children tend to go in and out of grief.

- Teens can be more challenging as they want to be accepted
  by their peers, and peer support is often their lifeline.
  Teens don't necessarily want their peers to know their true
  feelings; they want to appear strong and confident. During
  adolescence, their moods are all over the place.

- Make sure that your teens know they can talk with you or
  that there is a supportive adult they can talk with.

- If your teen is willing, ask him or her what friends might
  be the most understanding. Suggest they just share their
  feelings with those friends. It is important that teens have
  positive outlets.

- Additionally, both children and teens can turn inward and
  pull away from friends. If you notice this, you need to address
  this with them. If they have difficulty expressing themselves,
  it might be helpful for them to get professional help.

Kate's Club helps build friendships

Helping Your Children Manage School While Grieving

 "Grief is a wound that needs attention in order to heal."

-Judy Tatelbaum

Kate's Club staff educates school counselors and teachers around the issues of grief. Kate's Club has a division, Kate's Club connects, that works almost exclusively in schools to provide grief support. We feel this is extremely important because children may spend most of their day in schools, so changes may be evident to teachers and counselors first. Parents, too, often have many questions related to how to help their children balance their grief while handling all the challenges of school.

You may see or teachers may report

- Decline in grades.
- Improved grades—sometimes you may see your child focus on being an overachiever in school.
  - At first glance, this does not seem like a worry, but sometimes we see grieving teens especially become overly focused on achievement to either distract from having to think about the loss or to try to make the deceased proud.
  - There can also be a drive toward perfectionism, which can create internal or external stress for the teen.
  - It will be important to keep an eye on this behavior.
- Behavior changes at school. You may get reports that your child is acting out in school.

- Distraction in class or when doing homework.

- School avoidance. Younger children may cry about being away from you, while older children and teens may try other tactics to avoid school.

- Somatic complaints: stomach or headaches to avoid school. The complaint may be related to the anxiety of going to school. When in school, your child may visit the school nurse frequently.

How to help

Communicate with school staff, including counselors and teachers.

- Communicate before child returns to school after a death.

- In addition, communicate anytime a child changes schools or even with new teachers every year.

- Children and teens revisit grief, so teachers may see grief reactions years after a loss.

- Work with teachers to adjust your children's/teen's workload. You may have to be a strong advocate.

- When at home, if homework is a struggle, try putting in timed breaks and snacks.

- Sometimes they just need to get some energy out; give them ten minutes to run outside or ride their bike around the block.

- If your child seems to need a break during class, work with the teacher to come up with a signal your child can use, so the teacher knows they need to step out or visit the counselor.

- Ideas include doing a thumbs-up or tugging at their ear. This way, the break will not bring attention to the child.

- Check in with teachers. Ask how your child is doing in class.

Watch for grief triggers

Children's literature and young adult literature are full of loss, including parent and sibling deaths. Reading those books could either be helpful for a grieving child as they may identify with characters or the reading may be an unwelcome trigger for grief.

- Check in with your child about how they feel about the reading assignment.
- Discuss alternative assignments with the teacher.

Other grief triggers could come up when performing in a play or watching films that include death. Again, discuss with your child their feelings around the situation.

For children, days at school that focus on interaction with parents such as "Donuts with Dads" or "Muffins with Moms" can trigger their grief and make them feel different than their peers.

- Plan and ask your child if they would like to bring someone in their life who helps fill the role of mom or dad. They may decide to skip it but let them make that decision.

Kate's Club teaches coping skills

Reflections

♥ Think of other aspects where you had to be resilient and were successful!

Chapter Six

Revisiting Grief Across the Lifespan

"Grief is as much about the future as the past."

-Grief Specialist Joshua Rosenthal

Helping Your Children Through the Years

In American culture, we tend to see grief as an event, when in fact, it is a journey. Children especially will revisit early loss throughout their lives. At each new developmental stage, children, teens, and even adults may revisit their grief. We sometimes call this "re-grieving." Remember, what happens to someone when they are five years old will look very different to that person when they are ten. As children see their peers having relationships with parents or siblings, they may miss the relationship with the person who died even more. Milestones and special occasions may trigger grief. At Kate's Club, we often hear girls and boys of all ages lament that their mothers or fathers won't be able to celebrate their graduation, marriages, or other important life cycle events. The following are some ways to support your children as they revisit grief throughout their lives.

Continuing Bonds

At Kate's Club, we believe that it is important to help our children/teens and families stay connected to the person who has died. The following are ideas on how to do so:

- Talk about the person who died. Share stories and memories in a casual way throughout your children's lives.

- Save special mementos from the person. Let children choose keepsakes from the person. If they are very young, keep things for them that reflect the person. Even if a parent died when your child was young, your child may find as a teen that they want to wear old concert T-shirts of the person who died.

  - Lane's daughter who is a young adult now wears her father's skateboard shirt.

  - They may want to save special items from a sibling even if the sibling was a baby.

- Keep them connected to family and friends of the deceased. Do your best to foster relationships with in-laws, other grandparents, and old friends (of the deceased). Children appreciate staying connected and getting to know their person from a different perspective. Encourage these friends and family members to share stories and pictures.

- Over time, check in and talk about the person when milestones happen. For example, how can you include the person in a wedding or graduation?

- Do something you enjoyed doing with the person who died and invite a close friend to join in with you.

- Plant a tree or bush in your loved one's honor. And perhaps on the anniversary of your loved one's death, make a point to sit by the tree or bush and reflect on your memories. You may also consider adding additional plants or flowers each year.

- Light a candle. Jewish people often light a Yarzieght candle on the anniversary of the death of their loved one. It is a candle that can be bought in most grocery stores in the ethnic section of the store and burns for twenty-four hours.

- Visit the grave or the place where scattered the ashes.

- Celebrate a holiday that the person who died enjoyed. For example, you may light sparklers on the Fourth of July because your son who died loved them. Or watch the Fourth of July fireworks in his honor.

- Donate to an organization in honor of the memory of the person who died on the person's birthday or day she died.

- Honor your person who died by telling heartwarming or funny stories.

- Call up someone who loved the person who died and just share together. (Another loved one may be struggling, too).

- Avoid using the person's memory to shame or guilt your child. Saying: "Would your mother be proud of you for doing that?" or "What would your father think?" when children or teens misbehave is not helpful.

Meaning Making

> ♥ "Grieving mindfully, means approaching your grief as an opportunity to grow by actively giving meaning to your pain."
>
> -Dr. Sameet Kamur

Loss is something that happens to us; meaning is what we make happen. Finding a way to create meaning out of the death doesn't necessarily erase suffering, but it can help us heal and grow.

You and your child(ren) may find meaning by honoring the person's life by helping others.

- For example, Lane's daughter volunteers with Camp Kesem, which provides camp to children affected by a parent's cancer.

- Other families have become involved in suicide prevention or organizations such as MADD.

- One family at Kate's Club founded an organization to help kids who could not afford to play lacrosse after their son who loved lacrosse died after being struck by a car.

Many people who experience early loss say that they have a greater appreciation for life and living in the present. Practice being mindful of moments and teach your children to do the same.

David Kessler, an expert on grief, often asked his clients, "What would be the best way to honor the years the person did not get?" Reflect on this question and ask your children their thoughts.

Grief Triggers Throughout Your Life

Your child will experience bursts of grief throughout their lives. At times, you may not relate it to the death. Young children are not able to fully process a major loss and may not until adolescence or beyond. Sometimes they may not recognize what they are feeling is grief and it may manifest as risky behavior in addition to expected teen rebellion. Keeping communication open and finding support for them is crucial. Find a therapist skilled in grief work.

- When children experience the death of a parent, grandparent, or older sibling, they may feel as though they miss out on validation from that person as they mature. Often, they will have the thought, "Would this person be proud of me?"

- Subsequent losses may re-trigger grief from an earlier death. Many families who phase out of regular Kate's Club programs will return when another death occurs in the family.

- Reaching the age of the parent or sibling when they died or having children of your own may bring a fresh awareness.

  One of Kate's Club's most active Buddies (volunteers) admitted she experienced a new wave of grief when she turned 24. Her older brother died at the age of 24 when she was 17. She faced a greater recognition that her older brother was very young.

- Children can only grieve at the time of the death based on their developmental ability, so it makes sense that they will need to reprocess a death as they reach new stages of development. Children who lose infant siblings may always wonder what it would be like to have that sibling with them throughout their lifetime.

- Children may have more questions about the death as they grow older. Remember as we said earlier to talk about the death in age-appropriate ways. As children grow older, the explanations and the way you talk about the death can mature as well. When they're older, they may want more details of the death to better understand.

Coping with the Holidays and the Anniversary of the Death of the Person

The holidays, special occasions (anniversaries, birthday of deceased), and the anniversary of the death of your loved one can evoke a great deal of mixed feelings and emotions. After the death, it may feel as if your life has come to an abrupt halt. You can feel frozen in time. In this next section we will address each of these life events and provide tips, suggestions, and ideas to help you cope with more ease.

The Holidays

The holidays can be the toughest times of the year with all the hustle and bustle, parties and socializing, holiday music, and festive decorations that are all supposed to bring joy. At the same time, the holidays can be painful reminders and magnify the death or loss. They are sentimental times that may bring back happy or even sad memories and pull at your heartstrings.

Holidays reinforce how things have changed. They mark a passage of time. In addition, the disruption of routines during the holidays as kids are out of school or you travel out of town may bring different feelings up for individual family members. Routines often distract us from our feelings of grief.

Family members may have different expectations. Most children are still very excited about the holidays, though they may move in and out of excitement and sadness.

Preparing Ahead of Time for the Holidays

The following are some questions that might help you figure out what is best for you and your family. As you read through these questions, it might be helpful to write down your answers. Writing down your answers can help you gain some clarity. There are no right or wrong answers; focus on what is best for your family!

Where am I in the grieving process?

- Where are my children/teens in their grieving processes?
- How will we engage in the holidays without the person who died?
- Will we ever be able to enjoy the holidays again?
- How can I still bring joy to my children's holidays when I am so sad?
- As parent or spouse, will the pain I feel around the holidays and other celebratory events ever go away?
- How will I muster up the energy to celebrate?
- What if I am looking forward to the holidays because they can provide a distraction from my family's pain and sadness? Is it okay to feel that way?
- How will you handle people telling you how you should celebrate the holidays?

♥ How can I still bring joy to my children's holidays when I am so sad?

Kate's Club holiday event

Issues to Be Aware of as You Cope with the Holidays

Acknowledge your feelings and your family members' feelings.

- The first few years after the death, the holidays are going to feel uncomfortable, and you may experience some conflicted feelings for many years. However, you will not always feel the way you feel right now!

- Adults must first wrestle with their own sadness and realize it is normal to feel sad on what is supposed to be a joyful day. Do your best to balance sharing your own sadness with finding the emotional energy to support your children's joy for the holidays.

- You may feel your mood is all over the place; understand that is very normal.

- Realize when the holidays approach that you may feel like you are regressing back to when the death first occurred. This too is normal.

- You may find that you feel angry at the person who died for leaving you to celebrate without him or her.

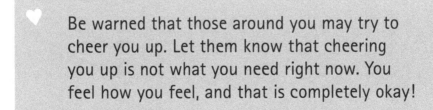

Be warned that those around you may try to cheer you up. Let them know that cheering you up is not what you need right now. You feel how you feel, and that is completely okay!

Plan and think about how you want to spend the holidays with your family. (If you had a child or teen die, this can be excruciatingly painful.)

- Prioritize. You don't have to do everything you used to do! Do you really have to send the Christmas cards or bake the usual cookies?

- Divvy up the tasks that are needed to be done. Ask for help.

- If you need help with the holiday decorations, ask for it. Don't think you have to do it all yourself.

- Order a prepared holiday meal. You don't have to cook the meal. Maybe just consider cooking one special food if you are up to it.

- You can say no to holiday invitations. Set realistic expectations and boundaries for yourself. For example, you can say, "Thank you for the invitation. I am not sure if we will come or not." Or, "I am grateful for the invitation, but for this year, we will not be attending." You don't have to say yes when you really mean no.

Consider how you honor your children's/teens' desire to celebrate the holidays.

- You might start by asking them how they want to celebrate the holidays. (Be prepared for a variety of opinions and mention to them you will try to honor them.)

- Let your children/teens know that the holidays may feel quite different this year. Assure them you will do your best to find ways to celebrate as a family.

- Your children may be used to having their other parent shop with them for a present for you. Ask someone to take them. Do not underestimate how important this may be to your children.

- If your children/teens would like to celebrate the holidays in their own special way to honor the memory of the person who died, make room for that, too.

- Remember children and teens tend to move in and out of their grief and sadness more easily than adults do. For example, one minute they can be very sad and the next want to go buy the Christmas tree, then get sad again and wonder how they will put up the tree without dad.

- While your children/teens may have the energy or spirit to celebrate, you may not. This is when great courage and strength is needed. While finding a way to celebrate is not easy (is in fact one of the more difficult things you will have to do), most parents say they do find a way to celebrate with their children/teens and get through the holidays.

Holiday Traditions

The grief journey calls upon you to re-examine and re-consider your holiday traditions.

- At Christmas time, if you used to drive around and look at the lights, because your wife loved this ritual, you might want to still do that with your children and share memories of the times you enjoyed looking at the lights together.

- After the death of a child, it may be especially painful to think of not hanging a stocking. Hang the stocking. Perhaps, if your child had a love of animals fill the stocking with donations to a particular organization in their honor.

- On the holiday, wear the color of an article of clothing that was special to the person who died.

- Listen to some favorite songs of the person who died on the birthday or holiday.

- Think about creating some new traditions that can be meaningful to you and your family. Some families start to do new activities in the first year or two after the death, and they become new family traditions.

- Lastly, remember there is no single right way to experience the holidays! The ways you celebrate will most likely change over the years.

Our hope is that you will be able to either combine old traditions with new ones or create new rituals that provide ways to enjoy celebrations and holidays.

Special Life Events

- Put a picture of your person on a graduation hat.

- Have a picture on a memorial table at a wedding.

- Wear a piece of your person's jewelry at a wedding.

- Eat a favorite food of the person who died at a special life event. For example, on July Fourth, Nancy would always celebrate by eating a hot dog, which her father loved to do.

Acknowledging the Anniversary of the Death of the Person Who Died

The first anniversary of the person's death can be particularly difficult. You may have experienced many firsts since the death, yet the first anniversary is unlike no other first.

- For many spouses or parents, your grief may return with surprising intensity. Some grief professionals have even named it, "anniversary grief." The intense grief you may experience is often the result of the significant relationship you had and how much the person meant to you and your family.

- You may experience a variety of feelings, including sadness. Many adults notice that a few weeks before the anniversary of the death and possibly a few weeks after you may experience mood changes.

  - You may experience a sense of sadness, a sense of emptiness, angry outbursts, anxiety, difficulty with concentrating, and crying outbursts.

  - You may also experience physical symptoms, such as headaches, sleep disturbances, and changes in appetite.

- Children, especially younger children, may not realize that the first anniversary of their sibling or parent's death has approached. As the supporting adult, you will need to determine whether you feel it's appropriate to remind your children about the anniversary.
    - Keep in mind that there are many ways to help your children remember the person without formally acknowledging the day the person died.
    - As your children grow older, you may be more inclined to remind them of the anniversary of the death, or they may even ask you.
    - If you decide to honor that day, consider asking your family how they want to spend the day.
    - Be mindful of what memories you choose to share and remember on that day. There may be some memories you will want to leave behind and others that are rich and special.
    - It's important to remember that the anniversary of your loved one's death is unique to you and your family.
- Lastly, many families ask, "How long do we acknowledge the anniversary of the person's death?" That question is one that each individual family will decide.
    - For many families, the anniversary of the death will remain as a touchstone memory.
    - And other families will not want to acknowledge the anniversary of the death.
    - It is perfectly OK if you decide as a family not to do so. Some families would rather recognize the birthday, or wedding anniversary, instead of the day the person died.

Connections with the Person Who Died

There are some children, teens, and adults, who will feel their loved one's spirit or presence through symbols, such as seeing a dragonfly or butterfly or something else that feels like they are present. People often feel embarrassed about expressing these experiences to others, but for many they feel very real and incredibly powerful.

 Some people feel their loved one's spirit or presence through symbols or something else that feels like they are present. For many they feel very real and incredibly powerful.

The following are some examples:

- A wife reported that every morning (her husband who was deceased) would visit her. She knew it was him, because the dancing musical wind-up ballerina he gave her long ago would dance and music would play.

- A wife shared that every time she would visit the grave of her husband, a dragon fly would visit.

- A teenager mentioned when he would go on favorite hike that he and his father had done together, he could sense his father's presence.

- A child looks at the clouds in the sky and sees her father and talks to him.

It's important to not dismiss these experiences or feel like there is something wrong. They can be a part of the grieving process and can help people feel connected to their loved one.

Dreams

After a loved one has died, adults, children, and teens, may dream about the person who died. Dreams play an important part in healing. At night when you are asleep, you tend to be most relaxed. Your unconscious mind is freer to process emotions that perhaps you may try to avoid when you are awake.

- You may wake up feeling as if the person you saw the person who died or that he/she may still be alive. Dreams of the deceased person can occur frequently and can help in the healing process.

- They have found that people who remember their dreams are most apt to dream about their deceased love one.

- People report they have visitation dreams in which the deceased spends time with the bereaved.

- A message dream you receive a message from the deceased, often telling you he/she loves you.

- A reassurance dream- where the bereaved receive a message of comfort or something positive.

- Sometimes the message is a warning or guidance.

- A traumatic dream can occur when you experienced something distressing and disturbing, such as a murder, suicide, or accident. Your dreams may be troubling where the person or you are angry or arguing. Dreams may reflect any complications or conflict you had when the person was alive.

The bottom line, it's important to not dismiss these dreams. They can be helpful in your grieving process. However, if they seem to get in the way of your healing, then it's important to seek out professional help.

Reflections

♥ Think about the new ways you will celebrate the holidays and honor the memory of your loved ones. Write them down so you can remind yourself of the positive steps you are taking.

Appendix

Books

Parents and Guardians

- *A Healing Place: Helping Your Child Find Hope and Happiness After the Loss of a Loved One*, Kate Atwood, founder of Kate's Club

- *Finding the Words: How to Talk with Children and Teens About Death, Suicide, Funerals, Homicide and Cremation*, Alan Wolfelt Ph.D. Companion Press, The Center for Transition and Loss

- *Grief is a Journey: Finding Your Way Through Loss*, Kenneth Doka, Atria Books

- *The Group: Seven Widowed Fathers Reimagine Life*, Donald Rosenstein, and Justin Yopp

Children

- *The Invisible String,* Patrice Karst
  A wonderful story that focuses on how love lives on after death.

- *When Dinosaurs Die: A Guide to Understanding Death*, Laurene and Marc Brown
  A comprehensive book, in a cartoon format, which discusses different issues related to death.

- *Always and Forever,* Alan Durant
  A story about losing someone close and how sharing together helps.

- *Sad about Sammy,* Valette Soppe and Tonya Southwick
  A family resource guide for children experiencing sibling loss.

- *The Scar,* Charlotte Moundlic
  The story of a boy who loses his mother. This book captures the loneliness of grief and provides hope that the deepest wounds can heal.

- *A Wrinkled Heart*, Tracy Hoexter
  A story about learning to be kind.

Tweens and Teens

- *Daddy's Climbing Tree*, C.S. Adler
  An 11- year-old and her family cope with the death of her father.

- *Fire in My Heart, Ice in My Veins: A Journal for Teenagers Experiencing a Loss*, E. S. Traisman

- *Straight Talk About Death for Teenagers*, Earl Grollman
  A book for teens explaining feelings and emotions they may have after a death.

- *There Are Two Kinds of Terrible*, Peggy Mann
  After his beloved mother dies of cancer, a boy must learn to relate to his father who has withdrawn into his own shell of suffering.

- *Love You Forever*, Robert Munsch
  A story about a son and his mother, that who go through life changes and passing on of rituals.

Websites

- David Kessler
  www.grief.com

- Center for Loss and Life Transition, Alan Wolfelt
  www.centerforloss.com

- National Alliance for Grieving Children
  www.children.org

- Compassionate Friends
  www.compassionatefriends.org

- Bereaved Parenting
  www.bereavedparenting.org

- Good Grief, The whole Child Initiative
  https://good-grief.org/the-whole-child-initiative/
  (Putting the good in grief)
- What's your grief
  www.whatsyourgrief.com
- Twins and Grief
  www.twinlesstwins.org
- Widow Strong
  www.widowstrong.com

Podcasts

- Grief for beginners
  www.npr.org/2020/05/12/854905033/grief-for-beginners-
  5-things-to-know-about-processing-loss
- Open to Hope Podcast
  www.Opentohope.com/radio
- The Widowed Parent Podcast
  on Apple Play or anywhere podcasts are hosted or at
  www.jennylisk.com

Blogs

- Grief Awareness blog Kate's club blog
  www.katesclub.org
- Grieving Dads to the Brink and Back
  www.grievingdads.com/blog/
- Open to Hope
  www.opentohope.com

Notes

Notes